T0191310

This MIT Kids Press book belongs to:

_____

_____

_____

To Ada, Lucien, Isabel, and Julian
AL

To my mother
RK

Text copyright © 2023 by Alan Lightman
Illustrations copyright © 2023 by Ramona Kaulitzki

All rights reserved. No part of this book may be reproduced, transmitted, or stored in an information retrieval system in any form or by any means, graphic, electronic, or mechanical, including photocopying, taping, and recording, without prior written permission from the publisher.

The MIT Press, the ☰ mit Kids Press colophon, and MIT Kids Press are trademarks of The MIT Press, a department of the Massachusetts Institute of Technology, and used under license from The MIT Press. The colophon and MIT Kids Press are registered in the US Patent and Trademark Office.

First US paperback edition 2024

Library of Congress Catalog Card Number 2022908694
ISBN 978-1-5362-2333-0 (hardcover)
ISBN 978-1-5362-3385-8 (paperback)

24 25 26 27 28 29 CCP 10 9 8 7 6 5 4 3 2 1

Printed in Shenzhen, Guangdong, China

This book was typeset in Alice.
The illustrations were created digitally.

MIT Kids Press
an imprint of Candlewick Press
99 Dover Street
Somerville, Massachusetts 02144

mitkidspress.com
candlewick.com

Isabel and the Invisible World

illustrated by

Alan Lightman   Ramona Kaulitzki

mit Kids Press

Isabel always wanted to see invisible things.

Isabel's friend Genevieve said she
had an invisible pet rabbit, which
she took for walks.

Isabel had two pets herself, Lola and Milly.

But she could see them.
She wanted to see invisible things.

Isabel had a birthday coming up.
She was going to be six!

"What do you want for your birthday?"
Isabel's mother asked. "You're a big girl now.
You deserve a special present."

"Would you like a new bicycle?" asked Isabel's mother. "Your old one is broken."

Isabel shook her head no.

"Would you like a toy castle?" asked Isabel's father.

Isabel shook her head no.

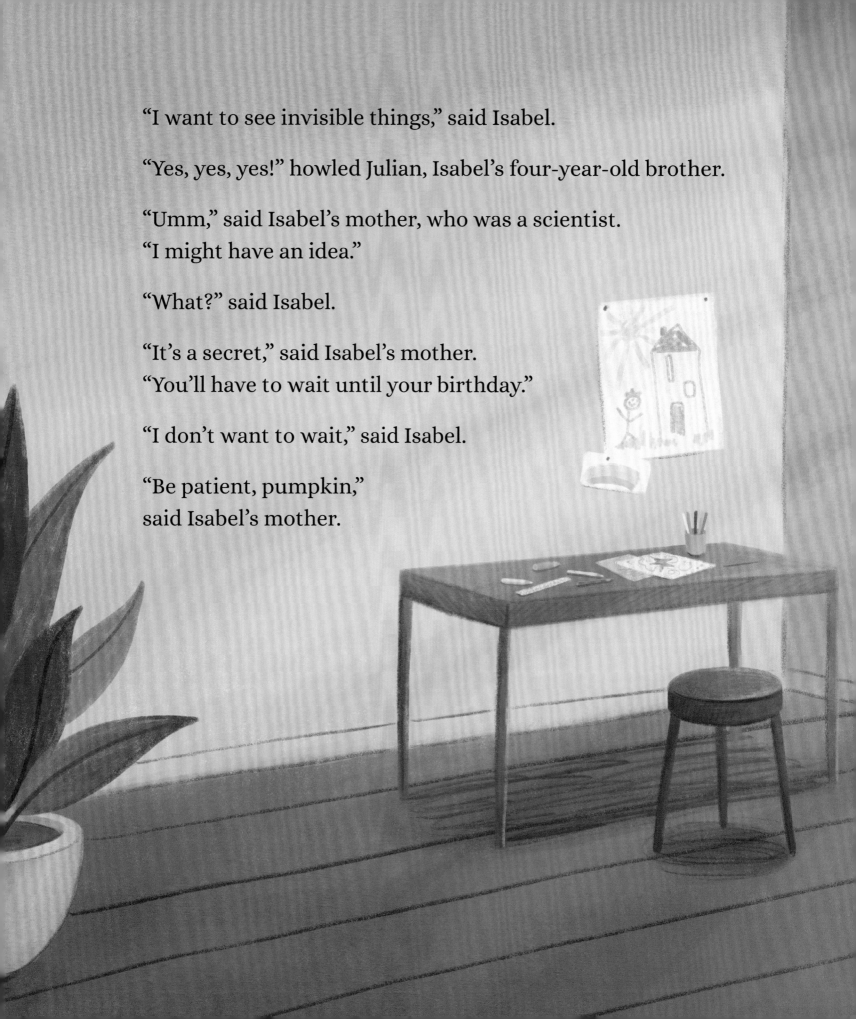

"I want to see invisible things," said Isabel.

"Yes, yes, yes!" howled Julian, Isabel's four-year-old brother.

"Umm," said Isabel's mother, who was a scientist.
"I might have an idea."

"What?" said Isabel.

"It's a secret," said Isabel's mother.
"You'll have to wait until your birthday."

"I don't want to wait," said Isabel.

"Be patient, pumpkin,"
said Isabel's mother.

Isabel began planning her birthday party.

She decided to invite her parents, her brother, Lola and Milly, and Genevieve and her pet rabbit.

Isabel made posters announcing her birthday. She put them around the house and in the yard.

"Let me help you with that," said Isabel's mother.

"No, thank you," said Isabel.

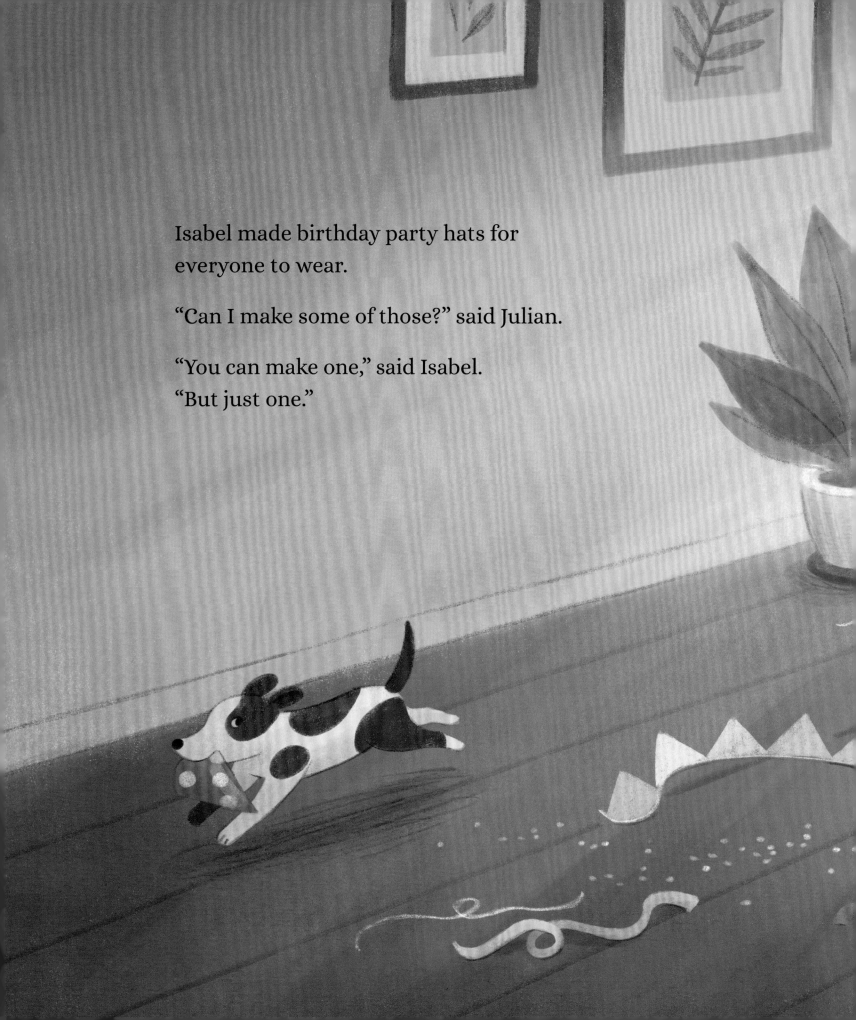

Isabel made birthday party hats for
everyone to wear.

"Can I make some of those?" said Julian.

"You can make one," said Isabel.
"But just one."

All the next week, Isabel couldn't think about anything except what her birthday present might be. And how cool it would be if she could see invisible things.

Finally, Isabel's birthday came around.

When she was finished eating cake, Isabel said, "Mommy and Daddy, I've been waiting a whole week for my special present."

"Here it is, pumpkin," said Daddy.

"What is it?" asked Isabel.

"It's a prism," said Isabel's mom.
"It lets you see invisible things.
Watch."

"Wow!" shouted Genevieve.

"Yay! Yay!" hollered Julian.

"Look at all the colors!" said Isabel.

"All those colors were invisible before," said Isabel's mother. "Now you can see them."

"What makes it do that?" asked Isabel.

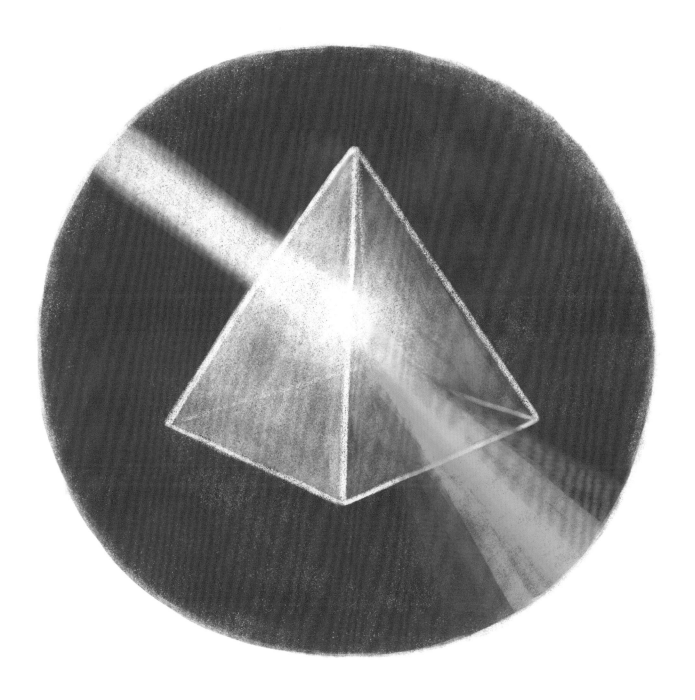

"Light is made of lots of colors," said Isabel's mom.
"You can't see them because they're mixed together.
The prism separates the colors."

"I wish I could see those colors all the time," said Isabel.

"There are even colors of light redder than red,"
said Isabel's mother. "They're called radio waves."

"I want to see radio waves," said Isabel.

"Your eyes can't see radio waves, even with a prism," said Isabel's mom. "But they're around us all the time, traveling through the air."

"I wonder what other invisible things there are," said Isabel.

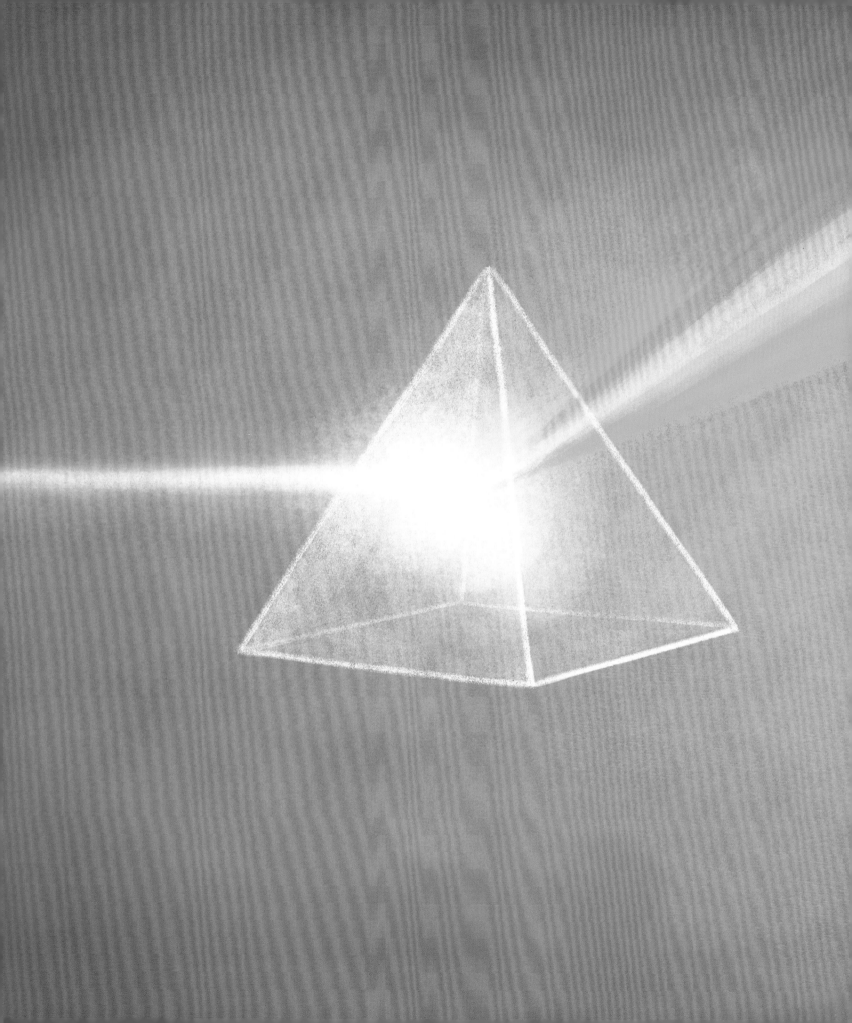

The Invisible World

Light is energy traveling through space. The energy comes in waves, like waves on a lake. Most light, including the light from the sun, has waves of many different lengths, from very short waves to very long waves. Blue light has a short wave. It would take about 53,000 waves of blue light to stretch one inch. Red light waves are a little longer. It would take about 36,000 waves of red light to stretch one inch.

When light goes through a prism, it changes direction. Waves of different lengths change direction by different amounts, causing the different colors to spread out.

The human eye can see light waves of only certain lengths, between blue and red. Radio waves are light waves with lengths longer than red light. There are also light waves with lengths shorter than blue light, such as ultraviolet, X-rays, and gamma rays. Our eyes cannot see radio waves or X-rays, but scientists have built machines that can detect them.

ALAN LIGHTMAN is a physicist, educator, and acclaimed author for children and adults. His debut picture book, *Ada and the Galaxies*, was published by MIT Kids Press and illustrated by Susanna Chapman. He is also the best-selling author of *Einstein's Dreams*. Alan Lightman has a PhD in theoretical physics and is a professor of the practice of humanities at MIT. He lives in Massachusetts.

RAMONA KAULITZKI is the illustrator of many books for children, including *Winter Lullaby* and the #1 *New York Times* bestseller *Sisters First*. When she's not illustrating, she can be found somewhere outdoors or at the riding stable. Ramona Kaulitzki lives in Potsdam, Germany.